Miniature Horses

by Natalie Lunis

Consultants:

Dianne Crittenden, Breeder and Founder of Mountain Side Miniature Horses,
Member of the American Miniature Horse Association,
American Miniature Horse Registry, and Western Canadian Miniature Horse Club

Cathy Buehrer, Amazing Sonrise Miniatures, Glasford, IL

BEARPORT PUBLISHING

New York, New York

Credits

Cover, © Juniors Bildarchiv/Alamy and Lilac Mountain/Shutterstock; Title Page, © Juniors Bildarchiv/Alamy; TOC-L, © Allan Morrison/Shutterstock; TOC-R, © Lilac Mountain/Shutterstock; 4T, © Dianne Crittenden/Mountain Side Miniature Horses; 4B, © Dianne Crittenden/Mountain Side Miniature Horses; 5, © Dianne Crittenden/Mountain Side Miniature Horses; 6, © Tina Kunkle/TMK Photography; 7, © Gemma Giannini/Grant Heilman Photography; 8T, © Jean Michel Labat/Ardea; 8B, © The Bridgeman Art Library/Getty Images; 9, © Popperfoto/Getty Images; 10, © Daniel Johnson/Fox Hill Farm; 11T, © Bob Langrish; 11B, © Roger S. Duncan/rogerduncanphoto.com; 12, © clearviewstock/Shutterstock; 13, © Dusty Perin/Dusty Perin Photography; 14, © AP Images/The Guymon Daily Herald, Shawn Yorks; 15T, © AP Images/Toby Talbot; 15B, © Ken Pratt/Timberline Studios, LLC; 16, © Bob Pepping/Contra Costa Times/ZUMA Press; 17, © Tina Kunkle/TMK Photography; 18, © Bob Langrish; 19L, © Bob Langrish/Animals Animals Enterprises; 19R, © Bob Langrish; 20, © Michael Mauney/Time Life Pictures/Getty Images; 21, © Bob Langrish; 22T, © jodi mcgee/iStockphoto; 22B, © Juniors Bildarchiv/Alamy.

Publisher: Kenn Goin
Editorial Director: Adam Siegel
Creative Director: Spencer Brinker
Design: Debrah Kaiser
Photo Researcher: Daniella Nilva

Library of Congress Cataloging-in-Publication Data

Lunis, Natalie.
   Miniature horses / by Natalie Lunis.
      p. cm. — (Peculiar pets)
   Includes bibliographical references and index.
   ISBN-13: 978-1-59716-861-8 (library binding)
   ISBN-10: 1-59716-861-0 (library binding)
   1. Miniature horses—Juvenile literature. I. Title.

SF293.M56L86 2010
636.1—dc22

                              2009010379

For more information, write to Bearport Publishing Company, Inc., 101 Fifth Avenue, Suite 6R, New York, New York 10003. Printed in the United States of America in North Mankato, Minnesota.

122009
120109CG

10 9 8 7 6 5 4 3 2

Contents

A Big Star

Button was becoming a big star in western Canada. The tan **mare** with the long, silky **mane** had appeared on a popular afternoon TV talk show. She had also put on a bandanna to play the "Rock on Pony." As this flashy character, she starred in commercials and newspaper ads for a big **telecommunications** company.

Button

Button as the "Rock on Pony" ▷

Button was soon visiting local classrooms. Children got to pet her, hug her, and ask questions about her. Yet how had a horse been able to fit inside a school? That was easy. Button is a miniature horse. At three years old, she was fully grown—and not much bigger than a very large dog.

△ **Button visiting a school**

People often call miniature horses "minis."

Measuring Up

Even though Button played the "Rock on Pony," she is not a pony at all. Ponies are bigger than miniature horses like Button.

pony

miniature horse

According to the **American Miniature Horse Association**, a miniature horse can be no taller than 34 inches (86 cm) when measured from the ground to the **base** of the last hairs of its mane. Ponies, on the other hand, are up to 58 inches (147 cm) tall. Of course, regular-size horses are even bigger. They stand more than 58 inches (147 cm) tall. At that size, many are more than twice as big as minis!

base of last mane hairs

34 inches (86 cm) or less

An adult mini weighs 150 to 250 pounds (68 to 113 kg). Many regular-size horses weigh more than 1,000 pounds (454 kg).

ground

A Bit of History

Button's rise to fame began a few years ago, around 2004. Yet very small horses have been popular for a very long time. During the 1600s, members of royal families in Europe raised them and kept them as pets.

American Miniature Horses

◀ King Louis XIV of France (1638–1715) had his own zoo filled with unusual animals—including unusually small horses.

There are different **breeds** of miniature horses. They were developed at different times and in different parts of the world. In the United States, the American Miniature Horse officially became known as a breed during the 1970s.

Later, during the 1800s, people started putting the little animals to work. In Europe and North America, they were used to pull wagons through small tunnels in **coal mines**. Over time, however, machines took over the jobs that the small horses did. As a result, the little horses were no longer needed as working animals. Instead, they became family pets once again.

The little horses that worked in mines were called pit ponies. "Pit" is another word for a deep hole that is dug into the earth to get coal out.

Living Small

Big horses need a farm with lots of land so that they can run and play. Miniature horses also need space outdoors so that they can get enough exercise. Yet they don't need as much room. Instead of a farm, the little animals can live comfortably in a big backyard.

A miniature horse can live in a big backyard and still have enough room to roam.

Miniature horses also need **shelter**—but they don't need a lot. Because they grow thick winter coats, they can stay safe from strong winds and harsh weather with just a sturdy **shed** to run into.

◀ In the summer, a shed can protect miniature horses from the sun.

△ A mini is getting a snack inside her stall.

Many people have **stables** for their minis so that the small horses can spend time relaxing indoors inside their own **stalls**.

How Much Food?

Horses are grazers—animals that eat grass. When they are outside in a **pasture**, they graze all day long. During the winter or other times when the grass does not grow, their owners feed them hay, which is dried grass. They also give the horses **grains**, such as corn and oats, to eat.

Horses, including minis, eat nothing ▶ but grass and grain. Yet they are big eaters. That's why people use the expression "to eat like a horse."

Miniature horses eat the same kinds of foods that big horses do. However, they need much less because of their small size. A full-size horse eats a big bundle of hay, called a bale, in just a few days. It can take a mini one week to go through a bale. That makes miniature horse owners happy, since it means it costs a lot less to feed their little pets.

No matter what their size, horses need plenty of water to drink. The water has to be fresh and clean, or else the horses can get sick.

▲ **This mini is munching on some hay.**

Small in the Saddle

Miniature horses can be trained to do many of the things that big horses do. Can they be taught to take people horseback riding, however? They can, as long as the rider weighs less than 60 pounds (27 kg)—which means that the only riders who can saddle up are young children.

Children who ride miniature horses need to use small saddles and **bridles** that are sized to fit the little horses.

Miniature horses are easier to handle than big horses because of their small size. As a result, they can help children learn to do more than just ride. For example, children can learn how to **groom** and clean up after horses by working with their pint-size pets.

◀ Older people and disabled people also like being around miniature horses because they are easier to handle than big horses.

Brushing and other ▷ types of grooming help build friendship between people and horses.

In the Driver's Seat

Adults and older children are too big to sit on a miniature horse's back. However, they can still use one to go for a ride. How? They can drive a cart that is pulled by a mini—or even a pair of minis.

▲ Minis are strong. Most can easily pull one or two people in a cart.

Driving a horse-drawn cart is a fun and old-fashioned way to see the countryside. It can also be part of an exciting **competition**. At miniature horse shows, drivers and their horses are judged on how well they work together. The horse walks, **trots**, and even moves through an **obstacle course** while pulling its driver in a cart.

Minis also compete in jumping events at horse shows.

Baby Minis

If an adult miniature horse is half the size of a regular horse, how small is a baby miniature horse? It's 16 to 21 inches (41 to 53 cm) tall and weighs about 20 pounds (9 kg). That makes it smaller than a full-grown German shepherd.

Cute as they are, baby minis are not usually right for new horse owners. People who have never raised a horse before are better off getting older horses that have been trained by experienced owners.

Just like any kind of baby horse, a baby miniature horse is called a foal. It can stand, walk, and run in the first few hours of its life. Its training as a pet also starts early. One of the first things a mini foal must learn is to get used to being around people. So time spent petting and hugging isn't just fun for the tiny horse and its owners—it's a great learning experience, too.

◀ During the first six months of its life, a miniature foal stays close to its mother.

▼ Unlike a regular-size foal, a mini foal is small enough to be picked up.

The Right Pet for You?

"Look how cute!" That's what most people say when they see a miniature horse. It's easy to understand why someone would want to have one as a pet. Does the animal's small size mean that taking care of it is an easy job, though?

This woman enjoys reading at home with a mini on her lap.

Some miniature horse owners let their pets inside their houses. The little horses still need to spend most of their time outdoors, though.

In many ways, owning a mini is easier than owning a regular horse. You don't need to have a big farm, for example. You don't need to be a big, strong person to handle one either. Yet in other ways taking care of a mini is a big job. After all, a miniature horse is still a horse. It needs training, grooming, exercise, and care from a **veterinarian**. Just like any other pet, this lovable little friend depends on its owner to keep it safe, happy, and healthy.

Like big horses, miniature horses are happiest when they are with others of their kind.

Miniature Horses at a Glance

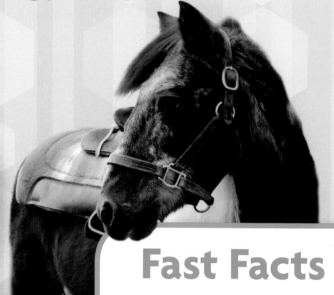

Miniature horses often serve as therapy horses. They visit schools, community centers, and senior citizen centers to cheer people up.

Fast Facts

Weight: 150–250 pounds (68–113 kg)

Height: 34 inches (86 cm) or less from the ground to the base of the last hairs of its mane

Colors: all the colors that full-size horses come in—including brown, black, white, and tan; also all the patterns that full-size horses come in, such as a main color with dark spots or patches

Life Span: 30 years or more

Personality: gentle, friendly, willing to please; able to pull carts, jump, and go through an obstacle course when properly trained; likes being around other horses

Glossary

American Miniature Horse Association (uh-MER-i-kuhn MIN-ee-uh-chur HORSS uh-*soh*-see-AY-shuhn) a group that is involved in many activities having to do with the American Miniature Horse breed, including providing new owners with information and setting rules for horse shows

base (BAYSS) starting point

breeds (BREEDZ) kinds of horses

bridles (BREYE-dulhz) the straps a horse wears on its head so that a rider can control it

coal mines (KOHL MYENZ) deep holes dug into the ground so that a rock-like fuel called coal can be dug out

competition (*kom*-puh-TISH-uhn) a contest

grains (GRAYNZ) seeds that come from plants and are used for food

groom (GROOM) to brush and clean

mane (MAYN) the thick, long hair on the head and neck of a horse

mare (MAIR) a female horse

obstacle course (OB-stuh-kuhl KORSS) a path set up with objects, such as cones and poles, that a person or animal moves through

pasture (PASS-chur) land set aside for animals to eat grass

shed (SHED) a small building

shelter (SHEL-tur) a safe place that covers or protects people or animals

stables (STAY-buhlz) buildings where horses or cows are kept

stalls (STAWLZ) small indoor places, usually in a stable or a barn, where horses are kept

telecommunications (*tel*-uh-kuh-*myoo*-nuh-KAY-shuhns) the science and technology that helps send messages over long distances by telephone, radio, cable, and other electronic means

trots (TROTS) moves in a way that is faster than a walk

veterinarian (*vet*-ur-uh-NER-ee-uhn) a doctor who cares for animals

Index

Bibliography

The American Miniature Horse Association. *Today's American Miniature Horse: The Horse for Everyone!* Alvarado, TX: The American Miniature Horse Association (2004).

Harris, Moira C. *America's Horses: A Celebration of the Horse Breeds Born in the U.S.A.* Guilford, CT: Lyons Press (2003).

Smith, Donna Campbell. *The Book of Miniature Horses: Buying, Breeding, Training, Showing, and Enjoying.* Guilford, CT: Lyons Press (2005).

Read More

Criscione, Rachel Damon. *The Miniature Horse.* New York: Rosen (2007).

O'Neal, Claire. *How to Convince Your Parents You Can Care for a Pet Horse.* Hockessin, DE: Mitchell Lane Publishers (2009).

Van Cleaf, Kristin. *Miniature Horses.* Edina, MN: ABDO Publishing Company (2006).

Learn More Online

To learn more about miniature horses, visit
www.bearportpublishing.com/PeculiarPets

About the Author

Natalie Lunis has written many nonfiction books for children.
She lives in the Hudson River Valley, just north of New York City.